15-Minute Finance

Get Control of Your Finances in 15 Minutes

Gregory Gooden

Foreword

This book is for all those who have been searching for a way to get in control of their finances but have been unable to find the right help. I am hoping this book helps shed some light on how you can manage your finances and put yourself on the track to financial success.

If you're ready, let's begin!

Table of Contents

How It All Got Started

15-Minute Finance began from a personal goal to read 1 book a week on any subject of interest. After getting started reading about topics such as managing personal finances, investments, and building wealth, I was hooked. The goal turned into a quest to improve my financial literacy and build a financially secure future, while still enjoying life. After talking with a bunch of people about how they approach personal finance and why we weren't taught this in school, I knew I wanted to share everything I have learned with the world. Fast forward several years later, I've coached countless people in building their financial foundation, improving their financial acumen, and living a better life because of their improved financial situations.

Introduction

Much to Learn, Not Enough Time

When someone says the words *personal finance*, people shudder. It is like a social taboo to discuss personal finances, much less how to manage them. This is a terrible thought process and one that dooms people to poverty. Now, I'm not saying you should talk about how much (or how little) money you have with random strangers, what I'm talking about is an open discussion on *how* we manage finances. The *how* is the important part because 1) it exposes us to the many different ways of achieving a similar goal (mind you, some people have terrible ideas about how to attain wealth), 2) it opens the dialog to what it means to acquire and maintain wealth, and finally 3) it allows those with the knowledge to help those without the knowledge.

15-Minute Finance is not meant to be a comprehensive manual on all things personal finance, hence the title, but it is meant to provide an overview of some of the major topics of personal finance. In each chapter, I won't go too in-depth for each area of personal finance, but I will give you enough information to understand how to get started. You should be able to read each chapter in this book in less than 15 minutes. Some areas may take a little longer if you are completely unfamiliar with a topic, but generally speaking, I've done my best to take the complicated junk out and put it in terms that everyone can understand. In each chapter, I will give you the answer you are looking for in as few words as possible. And in all cases, you can take what you learn and modify it to fit your needs. I am not trying to sell you on any specific company or product, and I will give you my best advice when it comes to maximizing your total return on investment. My end goal for you is to get you to a level of financial competency where you can understand how to make better, more informed, financial choices.

Chapter 1

Budgeting & Expense Tracking

Look, nobody likes to be told what and where to spend their money, but let's face it, if we want to accumulate wealth we need to plan for it. This doesn't mean you deprive yourself of the nice things in life, it just means that you either 1) plan for those nice things, or 2) cut back on the number of nice things you indulge in. Do you *need* that Grande double shot caramel frozen whatever, every single

7

day? The answer is NO (though I had a hard time following my own advice for about a year). This brings me to the point that you need to learn to live below your means, if you want to get on track to attaining wealth.

Since you've read this far, I know you are serious about acquiring wealth. This is what I want you to do. For one month, write down all of your expenses. Everything from your mortgage/rent to the $0.65 you spent for an overpriced candy bar. It may seem petty and unnecessary but hear me out first. After you have written down all of your expenses I want you to put them into the following categories: **Household Items, Utilities, Fuel/Parking, Car Insurance,**

Car Payment, Groceries, Eating Out, Mortgage/Rent, and Miscellaneous. Feel free to break any of the categories out to more categories, or not use categories that don't apply to you (e.g. if you don't own a car and instead ride a bicycle then either change the title to Bicycle Expenses or don't use the category at all).

Next, I want you to take a look at expenses and add them up by category. Everything in the **Eating Out** category should be added together, everything in the **Groceries** category should be added together, and you should do this for each applicable category.

Finally, see what categories really stick out in terms of how much you spent and how much you thought you spent. The fixed costs like housing you can't really change, but maybe you've been eating out a few too many times a week, and bought fewer groceries than you could have. What I want you to do is cut out enough of the "extra stuff" to get your expenses (not including housing and utilities) down to 30-40 percent of your take-home income.

That's it. Once you truly see how much you spend through tracking your expenses, you will have a much easier time cutting out all the excess. My advice is to do this every month until you get your expenses under 30 percent. I know this may be a challenge for some, but trust me when I say it will make a huge difference later on, especially when you start putting the excess into savings and investments. You may ask, "Well what about the other stuff, household expenses and savings... what should I spend on that?" My short answer is *read ahead*; my longer answer is to plan on spending 40-50 percent on housing expenses (Chapter 7), and 20 percent or more towards savings (Chapter 2) and investing (Chapter 4).

Chapter 2

Saving

Building an Emergency Fund

Do you have money saved for an emergency, such as a car repair, medical bill, or job loss? Be honest with yourself, I'm not in the business of judging people. If you do have money saved up, how much? Is it enough to cover all your expenses for two weeks? How about one month? How about two to three months? Did you know the average American doesn't have enough money set aside to cover a $1,000 emergency expense? That's a scary statistic, to say the least. If you don't fall into that category, great, you will still learn a lot from this chapter. If you do fall into this category, not great, but you will absolutely benefit from this chapter.

Step 1, assess your level of security. My personal recommendation is to have no less than six months of expenses in a savings account. If you can push it to twelve months then I consider that even better. This is an emergency fund, so it should cover you in an emergency such as a job loss and/or a car repair. My motto is *plan for the worst and hope for the best.* If you never need to touch the emergency fund then ok, but if you do (and only because of an emergency) then you'll be glad you have it.

Step 2, start saving a small amount. Don't try to push yourself too hard to save money. Start with saving $10-$25 per week and then increase it gradually to $50 per week over the course of a few months. The reason you want to increase it gradually is so that you don't feel the initial hit of less income, and you'll be able to adjust better.

Step 3, automate it, and forget it. You will need to setup automatic transfer with your bank to deposit money on a weekly/bi-weekly basis to a separate savings account. This will ensure that you don't forget and also, you won't spend what you don't see. Your bank can help you with this, so just call them up and tell them that you want to open a savings account and that you want money to be automatically transferred (for free) from your checking to savings.

Once you have saved enough to cover, at a minimum, 6 months' worth of expenses you can cut back on transferring money from your checking account to emergency fund. I wouldn't recommend stopping it all together, but you should certainly keep feeding your emergency fund to stay ahead.

Saving for a Short Term Expense

Along the same lines as the emergency fund, you'll want to save money towards known short term expenses. An example of this might be dental braces. We all know how much dental braces cost, and if you don't the answer is A LOT. So why not start preparing for the cost, before rather than after the fact. In order for you to save for a short term expense you will want to take the same approach as the previous section and automatically set money aside in a separate savings account for only that expense. Since this is a short term savings account, you want to be sure you don't put all your money towards this at the expense of funding your emergency savings fund. Emergencies are more important than luxuries.

What I want you to do is to open a savings account and name it Short Term Savings. Ideally, you want to have 5 percent of your annual salary (not take home pay) in this account. I know that seems like a lot of money, and it is, but this savings account will act as a buffer between your regular checking account and your emergency fund when it comes to expenses you are planning for.

Take for example someone who earns $55,000 a year in salary. If we divide that by 24 (assuming you get paid twice a month), before taxes you will want to save an average of about $115 per pay check. This is a lot of money to simply put away, and you don't need to have 5 percent in your account in one year, but the sooner you can get to that 5 percent mark, the more financially secure you will become.

My advice is to put as much towards your short terms savings as possible until you reach your goal, then cut back slightly on how much you contribute.

Chapter 3

Debt

Cutting the Credit Card Debt

If you've got credit card debt, then you know how hard it seems to pay it off. Every time you put money towards it, something else comes along to make the debt double in size. If you are only paying the minimum amount due, then you might be paying your credit card off forever, which is exactly what the credit card companies want you to do.

21

What you need to do is pay off your credit cards as quickly as possible. You are probably asking, "But how am I supposed to do that?" Well, I'm going to tell you. First and foremost, I will tell you my recommended plan for paying credit card debt off. It may not be the most efficient for some people, but all-in-all the end goal is the same - to pay off the credit card debt.

I want you to start paying off your credit card with the least amount of debt first. Forget about effective interest rate (for now) and remember, this is the short and sweet version. Your goal is to make small wins and compound those wins into a snowball effect.

You will accomplish this goal by continuing to pay the minimum amount due for all other credit cards, as you have been doing, and by paying any extra money you have towards this credit card debt. Once you have fully paid off that credit card, take that same approach and pay off the second credit card. Eventually, you will have paid off all your credit card debt and you will see yourself with a lot more money in your pocket.

This all goes without saying, you will need to reduce your spending for each credit card. You cannot, I repeat, cannot go back to spending money on the credit card you just finished paying off. You will only put yourself back into the same predicament. Worse, you will feel like you've done all this work for nothing.

Paying Off Your Auto Loans

Did you know that the average American household holds between $8,000 and $15,000+ in auto loans? Imagine, if you didn't have to pay a monthly expense to own your vehicle, what could you do with that money? I'd venture to guess that by now you know you should save it or pay off a debt somehow. But that's not the point of this section. The point of this section is to help you pay off your auto loan faster using a method that you will hardly notice.

The first thing I will assume is that you have automatic deduction for your car payment. If you don't, get it. It will make your life much easier. Next, I want you to take your monthly payment and split it in half. Finally, I want you to set up automatic bill pay to pay half the expense of your monthly auto loan every two weeks. For example, if you pay $300 per month for your auto loan, I want you to setup automatic bill pay to pay $150 every two weeks.

The reason I want you to do this is because, in a year, you will have made one additional payment, without even noticing. Think about it, if you pay monthly, you are making 12 payments per year, but if you pay every two weeks you will have made 13 total payments. Using this method will help you save hundreds, if not thousands, of dollars in interest you would have otherwise paid had you continued to pay monthly.

Tackling Student Loans

Let's face it, many of us have student loans that follow us for the majority of our lives. I am not going to go on a political rant about free tuition, but if you have no other means to pay for college and you took out a student loan, this chapter will help you get on track to paying it off early.

Since the average student debt is between $11,000 and $29,000, our focus will be slightly different than for paying off a credit card or auto loan, albeit, not a huge change in process, but enough that you will want to pay attention.

The first thing I want you to do is tell yourself "I will pay this student loan off early." Tell yourself this every single day. The next thing I want you to do is make sure you are out of credit card debt. The reason I say this is because the high interest rate of credit card will eat you alive if you try to focus only on student debt. So read up on the section about eliminating credit card debt again and make sure you have a solid plan for paying off credit card debt. Once you have all that under control, I want you to focus on making extra payments to the loan company. But, just paying more is not enough, you need to know and understand where and how that **additional payment** is applied. I want you to pay the minimum amount due each month. For all additional payments, I want you to contact the loan company and tell them you want to make a *principal only payment*. Trust me when I say this, if you just pay more each month the loan company will be sure to take a piece of that extra money and put it towards accumulated interest. This is not what your extra money should go towards, padding their pockets. This extra payment needs to go to the principal amount of the debt (i.e. the original loan amount).

The reason you want to do this is that if you just make extra payments without specifying, chances are you will waste a large portion of that money on future interest the loan company will charge you. It's as if they think you WANT to pay them more money than necessary. If you make *principal only payments* you are reducing the portion that the interest rate is affecting. In other words, instead of them charging you 3 percent on $10,000 ($300 simple interest), they would be charging you 3 percent on $9,000 ($270 simple interest). At first glance, that may not look like much, but remember that the loan has compound interest while I showed you simple flat interest in the example. The loan company would prefer you to keep a higher principal balance because it means that it gives the interest more time to compound, resulting in you paying more.

My recommendation is that direct any extra payments directly to the principal amount.

Chapter 4

Investing to Earn.
It's Not Scary

Some people will say that the stock market is risky and you shouldn't put any money into it. I say they are full of... junk. The stock market is one of the single most effective ways of attaining wealth. I won't bore you with the details but, the idea of not investing any money is only going to serve as a detriment to your future financial security.

How much should you invest? If you want to build wealth you should invest, at a minimum, 10 percent of your annual income in the stock market. This also includes 401k, 403b, and IRA accounts (Chapter 5). For this chapter, I want you to take a look at a couple of companies that offer low or no cost stocks.

First, I recommend Loyal3 as a stock purchasing platform. This company has a limited number of stocks you can purchase but all of them are free to buy and sell (i.e., no commission charges). I am a proponent of low cost index funds, but I also see a great value in purchasing individual shares of a company. I won't get into who you should purchase but I will say that I purchase stocks from companies that I patronize. If you are an Apple fan, you might want to look at Apple stock, if you love eating out at a restaurant that you believe has a potential for growth, then see if they have public stock on Loyal3. I also want to note that you don't need to buy the stock at the full price, you can buy partial shares. For example, if you don't want to spend $100 for one Apple share, then buy a piece of share for the fraction of the single share cost.

The thing I like best about Loyal3 is that you can setup monthly automatic buy orders. This is great because you can set it to purchase $20 of Amazon stock (for example) each month. You can check out Loyal3 at loyal3.com.

My second recommendation for you to invest through is Vanguard. If you don't want to buy individual stocks because you don't think you're a good stock picker, why not buy the entire stock market? This means that you will do as well as the entire market. Vanguard is the leader in low-cost index funds. I HIGHLY recommend you take this route as the stock market has historically averaged about a 7 percent yearly increase over time. I would recommend checking out all the available Exchange Traded Funds (ETFs) and making your own decision, but some of the low-cost ETFs that I recommend are the S&P 500 ETF (VOO), Total Stock Market ETF (VTI), and Growth ETF (VUG).

I'm not getting paid to endorse any of these companies (though if they wanted to send me a check, I wouldn't say no). I just wanted to give you some examples of who might be good to start with. Whichever option you chose, you want to put away, at a minimum, 10 percent of your income with the goal of putting away 20 percent or more. This falls in line with the 50-30-20 rule I mentioned in Chapter 1.

Chapter 5

Planning for Retirement

401k & 403b

If you work for a company that offers a 401k or 403b plan, then chances are they are offering you the ability to put money into a retirement account *pretax*. What this means is that you can contribute money to a retirement account and not be taxed on that contribution, for the time being. The key words being *for the time being*. The reason is, when you withdraw the money when you reach retirement age, you will need to pay tax on the amount you take out.

If your company matches your contribution up to a certain amount, ALWAYS, contribute at least that much. I know that may seem impossible or too difficult to do, but trust me, if someone offered to give you an extra $100 in any other way, I am sure you'd take it. Your company is essentially giving you free money if you match contributions to the max amount. If your company doesn't match your contributions, then look for a different company to work for. Just kidding!

My recommendation is that you should take a look at your expenses and try to contribute a minimum of 10-15 percent of your pretax income towards a tax-deferred retirement account. Each year, increase your contribution by 1 percent until you get to 20 percent or more. You will see over time your retirement balance increasing well above the contributions you make. This is when your money will be making money.

ROTH & Traditional IRA

Full disclosure, I am a proponent of ROTH IRAs. I max out my ROTH IRA and I have recommended to everyone that has worked with me to do the same.

The short reason behind this is that any gains are tax-free. Yes, you did hear me correctly, any gains earned from a ROTH IRA are tax free, assuming (of course) you withdraw money at retirement age. If you withdraw the **earnings** before retirement age, in most instances, you will have to pay a penalty. An additional benefit to the ROTH IRA is that you can withdraw the **contributions** you make at any time without penalty.

The opposite of the ROTH IRA is the Traditional IRA. This retirement account is similar to a regular 401k/403b plan. Money is contributed on a *pretax* basis and withdrawals (again made at retirement age), are taxed as regular income. If you already have a 401k/403b chances are you won't need a traditional IRA. When people move to a new job, in many cases they do something called an "account rollover," and move their retirement account from their previous employer to their new employer's retirement plan. However, there are some companies where this is not allowed. If you encounter this, my recommendation is that you take the money from your 401k/403b plan and roll it over into a traditional IRA (my preference is Vanguard). This will ensure that your money is in a safe place where you have control over it, rather than being subject to the whims of your previous employer.

My recommendation is that you should open a ROTH IRA and fund it as much as you can (to the max if possible). My preference is Vanguard for IRA accounts, and they have low-cost target date mutual funds to which you can contribute. Try to set up an automatic contribution on a bi-weekly basis, even if it's for only $20. Start with whatever you can manage and you will be amazed at how quickly it adds up. If you can, incorporate both the 401k/403b and ROTH IRA into your 20 percent contribution. What this means is, depending on your income, adjust your ROTH IRA and 401k/403b contributions to reach the contributions of at least 20 percent of your annual income.

Chapter 6
Saving for Education

The 529 Plan

The 529 education plan comes in two different flavors. The first is a pre-paid tuition option and it is as simple as it sounds. You pre-pay for the tuition at today's rate for a future time when you or your child will attend a college or university. You can certainly take this option if you know your child will go to a specific school, but many people consider the second option as the more economical choice.

The second option is to contribute *after-tax* money into a *tax-deferred* 529 plan. The reason it is considered *tax-deferred* is that, if you don't spend the earnings on IRS qualified educational expenses you will have to pay a withdrawal penalty in addition to paying taxes on the withdrawal.

This 529 plan is similar to a 401k or other retirement account, whereby you select a plan that has a certain percentage of stocks and bonds and as the markets increase so do the earnings in the 529 plan. An additional benefit of the 529 plan is that the government allows contributions to be made into this 529 plan from virtually anyone, including grandparents, friends, other relatives, etc. In addition, you can contribute up to $14,000 yearly towards the 529 plan.

The last benefit of the 529 plan is that, if your child gets a full scholarship, you can withdraw the money without having to pay the penalty, though you will still have to pay taxes on the earnings.

My recommendation to you is to check out Merrill Edge and their 529 plans. They have quite a few money allocation options and a number of plans that automatically adjust each year as the child gets closer to college age. My personal preference is to invest in a plan that automatically adjusts as each year passes, think of it as a target-date college fund, very similar to a target date 401k/403b retirement plan. This plan will keep much of the fund in stocks, in the earlier years, and as your child gets closer to college age it will slowly move towards a higher bond allocation.

Educational IRA

Although I am a fan of the 529 plan, it would be worth your time to also consider the Educational IRA (EIRA). With the EIRA, you are only allowed to contribute $2,000 annually. In addition, you can't contribute any more money after your child turns 18.

One of the benefits of an EIRA is that you can transfer the account to another beneficiary. Let's say, for example, your child decides to start their own business and not attend College. You can rename their sibling or another relative as the beneficiary.

My recommendation is to start funding a 529 plan now. Another option is to open an EIRA and start funding it now, and then, if you later decide that you want to contribute more money towards your child's education, you can start funding a 529 plan. In either case, it's important to start contributing as early as possible. If you don't have a child now you can still open and contribute to a 529 or EIRA for yourself and then switch the beneficiary over to your child once they are born.

The Last Resort

I am going to keep this chapter very short because I DO NOT RECOMMEND what I am about to tell you. The Government does allow you to use your personal ROTH IRA to fund your child's education, and not have to pay taxes on the earnings. This can be a very dangerous option because you will be diminishing your principal and therefore losing out on years of compounded interest. You can make the choice yourself, but you need to weigh the cost and benefit of sacrificing your future retirement for your child's education.

Chapter 7

Home Ownership

Buy What You Can Afford

I am not one to tell people how to be happy, especially when it comes to their money. But I can't help but wonder why people still buy houses that they can't afford. We've already seen the devastating effects of the housing crash, and many of those people who were affected could actually afford their homes. Many more of the people that were on the borderline of bankruptcy were completely wiped out. In any case, my recommendation is to not purchase a home that you can't afford.

So how do I determine how much house I can afford, you may ask? Luckily that's a simple-ish answer. The rule of thumb is that you should not spend any more than 40-50 percent of your gross annual pay on household expenses. These expenses include, mortgage, fees and additional costs associated with the purchase of the home, homeowners association fees, utilities, property tax, etc.... I think you get the point. The purchase of the home itself isn't the only thing to factor in. To be on the safe side, you don't want the value of your home to be more than three to four times your gross annual income. Now, I am sure many of you would consider such a suggestion to be outrageous, and if you do, well, don't take the advice then. But, which position would you rather be in? Owning a home that you know is affordable and within your price range or being at the mercy of the housing market with the potential for another housing market crisis. Some may argue differently, but buying your home shouldn't be a risky venture. I would much rather be safe than sorry, you can always sell your house, but not if it's taken by the bank.

Paying It Off Early

You have two options for paying off your home early. The first option is winning the lottery. The second option is to put more money towards the principal of the home loan. Since option one is highly unlikely, you will need to put more money towards the principal of the home loan. Note that I said the *principal* and not just the loan. The short and sweet reason is because banks like to take interest out of any and all money you pay towards your home loan, so it is important to be **specific** about where you want your extra payments to go.

Now, I don't want you to tell me you can't put more money towards the home loan; the simple fact is, you can't afford not to. You will end up paying thousands of dollars more in interest alone if you pay your loan in the typical 30 year period.

Are you ready to hear the secret? Step 1, choose a single month for which you will make one extra payment per year. Step 2, automate the process or remember to send in an extra check that month. It's as simple as that. If I made that seem complicated, here is the even shorter version. Make one extra mortgage payment per year. You would save thousands of dollars in interest just by following this strategy alone.

Chapter 8
Living the Rich Life

There you have it, as quickly as you started this book you've already finished it. I hope I was able to give you enough information to help you familiarize yourself with each topic. It should go without saying that this is not a comprehensive manual for managing all of your personal finances (that's in my next book). This book is meant to help you get a successful start in the major areas of personal finance. I am hoping there are some things in here that inspire or interest you.

Once you have a good grip on your personal finances (through the concepts you have learned in this book), you will see that you are able to live on slightly less than you did before and your bank account and retirement account will no longer be starved.

Remember, it's called *personal* finance for a reason. Until we meet again. Good luck and keep it short.